The
DINOSAUR
Alphabet Book

by Jerry Pallotta
Illustrated by Ralph Masiello

 Charlesbridge

To Anna Ginnetti and Pam Hansen, the best babysitters in the world.

The illustrations are dedicated to my daughter, Alexa, born June 14, 1990.

Published by
Charlesbridge Publishing
85 Main Street
Watertown, MA 02172-4411
(617) 926-0329

Library of Congress Cataloging-in-Publication Data
Pallotta, Jerry.
    The dinosaur alphabet book / by Jerry Pallotta; Ralph Masiello,
illustrator.
        p.   cm.
    Summary: Full of interesting facts, this alphabet book introduces
children to the fascinating world of dinosaurs.
    ISBN 0-88106-467-X (reinforced for library use)
    ISBN 0-88106-466-1 (softcover)
    1. Dinosaurs–Juvenile literature. 2. English language–Alphabet–
Juvenile literature.
[1. Dinosaurs. 2. Alphabet.] I. Masiello, Ralph, ill. II. Title.
QE862.D5P1383   1991
567.91 — dc20   90-83114
[E]   CIP
                                                                     AC

Printed in the United States of America
(sc) 15 14 13 12 11
(hc) 10   9   8   7   6   5

Printed on Recycled Paper

Books by Jerry Pallotta:
   The Icky Bug Alphabet Book
   The Icky Bug Counting Book
   The Bird Alphabet Book
   The Ocean Alphabet Book
   The Flower Alphabet Book
   The Yucky Reptile Alphabet Book
   The Frog Alphabet Book
   The Furry Animal Alphabet Book
   The Underwater Alphabet Book
   The Victory Garden Vegetable Alphabet Book
   The Extinct Alphabet Book
   The Desert Alphabet Book
   The Spice Alphabet Book
   The Butterfly Alphabet Book
   The Freshwater Alphabet Book
   The Airplane Alphabet Book
   Going Lobstering
   Cuenta los insectos (The Icky Bug Counting Book)
   The Crayon Counting Book

Ralph would like to thank Jessica and Jeremy Bancroft.

A a

A is for Ankylosaurus. This was one of the armored dinosaurs. The spikes sticking out of its back and sides were sharp. The club on the end of its tail could swing around and be used as a weapon. If you were a dinosaur, would you go near the Ankylosaurus?

B b

B is for Baryonyx. This fish-eating dinosaur had two large claws. Scientists cannot figure out whether the claws were on its front feet or its back feet. If the giant claws had been on its back feet, they would have bumped into its front legs when it walked. Its flat head was shaped like the head of a crocodile.

C is for Compsognathus. Not all dinosaurs were huge. The Compsognathus was no bigger than a chicken. Its feet were like those of many birds today. The Compsognathus had three toes pointing forward and one toe pointing backward.

D is for Diplodocus. This is one of the longest dinosaurs that anyone has found. Most of its length comes from its very long tail and very long neck. It was a gentle plant-eater.

Dd

The Diplodocus could have used its long tail like a whip to defend itself against the meat-eating dinosaurs.

E e

E is for Edmontosaurus. The Edmontosaurus was found near Edmonton, Alberta, Canada. It had over one thousand teeth in its strong jaws. If the Edmontosaurus were alive today, it would take a dentist about a week just to clean its teeth.

F is for Fabrosaurus. The Fabrosaurus was one of the dinosaurs that had hip bones like the birds that live today. Scientists divide all dinosaurs into two groups. One group has hip bones like birds, the other group has hip bones like lizards.

Ff

No one knows why dinosaurs became extinct. There are many theories. One theory is that a giant star, a supernova, exploded near earth and the radiation slowly killed off all the dinosaurs.

G g

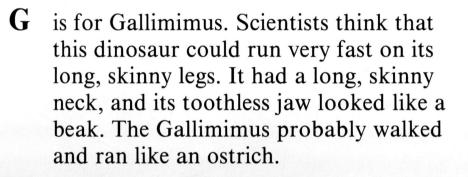

G is for Gallimimus. Scientists think that this dinosaur could run very fast on its long, skinny legs. It had a long, skinny neck, and its toothless jaw looked like a beak. The Gallimimus probably walked and ran like an ostrich.

H is for Heterodontosaurus. This dinosaur only grew to be about as tall as a first or second grade student. Most dinosaurs had either sharp meat-eating teeth or flat plant-eating teeth. The Heterodontosaurus was very unusual. It had three different types of teeth: sharp front incisors, pointed canines, and flat, grinding, back-teeth, just like you do.

H h

I i

I is for Iguanodon. This is the second dinosaur ever discovered. Someone noticed that it had teeth just like an Iguana and decided to call it an Iguanodon. The Iguanodon's thumbs were sharp spikes that it probably used to tear up leaves and branches for food.

J is for Jaxartosaurus. The Jaxartosaurus was one of the "duck-billed" dinosaurs. Dinosaurs existed millions of years before ducks so maybe it would be more appropriate to call ducks the "dinosaur-billed" birds.

J j

K k

K is for Kronosaurus. The Kronosaurus was a giant ocean-going reptile, but it was not a dinosaur. Many people think that the ocean-going reptiles were dinosaurs, but all dinosaurs had legs and walked on land. The Kronosaurus had flippers and swam in the ocean.

K is for Kentrosaurus. The Kentrosaurus had both bony plates and spikes sticking out of its back. The Kentrosaurus was small. Its spikes could have kept the giant dinosaurs from stepping on it. The name Kentrosaurus means "prickly lizard."

Another theory of why dinosaurs became extinct is that a giant meteor hit the Earth, and the dust from the collision blackened the skies. With no sunlight, the plants would have died and then the plant-eaters would have had nothing to eat. When the plant-eaters died off, the meat-eaters would have had nothing to eat, except maybe each other.

L is for Lambeosaurus. The Lambeosaurus was a duck-billed dinosaur that had a funny shaped head. Several other duck-billed dinosaurs had different shapes on their heads. Maybe the different shapes helped them tell each other apart.

L l

M is for Megalosaurus. This is it! This is the first dinosaur ever discovered. At first, people thought that the bones of the Megalosaurus were from an ancient giant horse, or an ancient giant rhinoceros, or hippopotamus. Eventually people realized that these bones were from a giant reptile, a dinosaur.

M m

Nn

N is for Nodosaurus. This armored dinosaur's tiny brain was probably no bigger than a golf ball or a walnut. The Nodosaurus did not have the long spikes that other armored dinosaurs usually had. The Nodosaurus had plating on its back that looked like hundreds of little buttons. Should it have been called a Buttonosaurus?

O is for Oviraptor. This dinosaur has a name that means "egg thief." The six foot tall Oviraptor went around eating the eggs of other dinosaurs. It probably crushed the stolen eggs with its strong toothless beak.

Oviraptors were not the only creatures stealing dinosaur eggs. Small mammals like rats also started eating the eggs of dinosaurs. This is another theory of why dinosaurs became extinct.

Oo

P is for Parasaurolophus. This dinosaur had a hollow bone growing across the top of its head. People used to think it was a snorkel that helped it breathe underwater. Now people think it may have been to make louder sounds or to smell things better. It may also have been a deflector to push aside branches and shrubs when the Parasaurolophus ran through the woods.

Pp

Q is for Questrosaurus. The Questrosaurus was a
long-necked plant-eater. Let's face it! No one
really knows what colors the dinosaurs were.
Anyone can make a good guess. Perhaps some
dinosaurs could change color the way some
lizards do today.

Q q

Maybe the Questrosaurus was red with blue stripes and yellow spots. Who really knows what color dinosaurs were?

R is for Ramphorynchus. Although this flying reptile lived during the time the dinosaurs lived on earth, it was not a dinosaur. No dinosaurs were able to fly. This creature should probably not be in a dinosaur book. Let's find a dinosaur that begins with the letter R.

Rr

Rr

R is for Riojasaurus. This dinosaur walked on all four legs and was a plant-eater. The Riojasaurus would have liked to eat broccoli, asparagus, lima beans, and spinach if there were any around millions of years ago. If you were a dinosaur, would you have eaten these vegetables?

What about cabbage, brussels sprouts, and cauliflower?

S is for Stegoceras. No, not the Stegosaurus. The Stegoceras was one of the boneheaded dinosaurs. The bone on the top of its skull was six inches thick. It was perfect for smashing into other boneheads or crashing into its enemies.

S s

T is for Torosaurus. This dinosaur had the largest skull of any known land animal. From the tip of its chin to the top of its collar, it measured nine feet long. Do you like horned dinosaurs? The Montanoceratops had a single horn on its head. The Torosaurus and the Triceratops had three horns. The Pentaceratops had five horns. The Styracosaurus was spectacular — it had horns all over its head!

T t

U is for "Ultrasaurus." This giant dinosaur has not yet been officially named. Only a few leg bones have been found. However, it is so huge that it probably deserves the name the "Ultimate Dinosaur." It is the largest found so far, unless, of course, you find one even bigger.

Uu

V is for Velociraptor. The Velociraptor is one of a group of dinosaurs that had a huge sharp claw on the front of each rear leg. This ferocious dinosaur may have been able to jump up onto other dinosaurs and attack them with its sharp curved claws. The fast-running Velociraptors probably hunted together in large groups.

V v

W is for Wuerhosaurus. Not much is known about this dinosaur and no one is really sure what it looked like. We do know it had rectangular shaped plates on its back.

No one really knows how many years old a Wuerhosaurus lived to be. Scientists say that some dinosaurs may have lived to be 200 years old. That is a lot of birthdays to celebrate.

W w

X is for Xiaosaurus. This dinosaur was discovered in China and therefore it has a Chinese name. The Xiaosaurus did not grow any taller than a person.

The Xiaosaurus and other dinosaurs may or may not have walked around in snow. Another theory of why the dinosaurs became extinct is that the Ice Age came and made the Earth too cold for the dinosaurs. If this is true, then why did crocodiles and alligators survive? Nobody knows.

X **x**

Y is for Yangchuanosaurus. The Yangchuanosaurus was a large, fierce meat-eating dinosaur. Its huge jaws, full of long saw-edged teeth, were good for stabbing and cutting. It was as tall as a three-story building. Wow!

Imagine this dinosaur walking down your street. Don't worry! The last dinosaurs lived about 65 million years ago. The last Yangchuanosaurus lived about 140 million years ago.

Y y

Z is for Zephyrosaurus. Look! There is a Zephyrosaurus skull. All over the world, there are zillions of dinosaur bones waiting to be discovered. The Zephyrosaurus has already been identified, but there are more new dinosaurs and fossils to find. Maybe some of them will end up with names that begin with the letter Z.

Z z